MW01041974

To:

_____

From:

_____

You're Invited
to Begin Your Christmas at:

Fort Macleod Alliance Church
1716 7a Avenue
403-553-4607
fmchurch@telusplanet.net

HERE IS LOVE,
THAT GOD SENT HIS SON, ...
HIS SON THAT NEVER OFFENDED,
HIS SON THAT WAS ALWAYS
HIS DELIGHT.

John Bunyan

CHRISTMAS
BEGINS WITH
Christ

Christmas Begins with Christ
Copyright © 2010 by Outreach Publishing

All rights reserved. No part of this book may be used or reproduced in any form or by
any electronic or mechanical means including information storage and retrieval systems
without permission from the author, except by a reviewer who may quote brief passages
in a review.

Outreach, Inc., Vista, CA 92081
www.outreach.com

Scripture quotations from THE MESSAGE. Copyright © by Eugene H. Peterson 1993, 1994, 1995,
1996, 2000, 2001, 2002. Used by permission of NavPress Publishing Group.
Scripture quotations from the NEW AMERICAN STANDARD BIBLE®, Copyright © 1960, 1962, 1963,
1968, 1971, 1972, 1973, 1975, 1977, 1995 by The Lockman Foundation. Used by permission.
Scripture quotations from The Holy Bible, New International Version® (NIV) ®, Copyright © 1973,
1978, 1984 by International Bible Society. Used by permission of Zondervan. All rights reserved.
Scripture quotations from the Holy Bible, New Living Translation, copyright © 1996, used by
permission of Tyndale House Publishers, Inc., Wheaton, Illinois 60189. All rights reserved.
Scripture quotations marked NKJV are taken from the New King James Version®. Copyright © 1982
by Thomas Nelson, Inc. Used by permission. All rights reserved.
Scripture quotations marked NCV are taken from the New Century Version of the Bible, copyright ©
2005 by Thomas Nelson, Inc. Used by permission.
Scripture quotations marked NRSV are taken from the New Revised Standard Version Bible,
copyright © 1989, Division of Christian Education of the National Council of the Churches of Christ in
the United States of America. Used by permission. All rights reserved.

ISBN: 978-1-9355-4128-8

Written by Rebecca Currington in association with Snapdragon Group, Tulsa, OK, USA.
Content from reDiscover Church is written by Kim Levings.
Cover and Interior Design: Tim Downs and Kathy Daubenspeck.

Printed in the United States of America

Dear Friend,

*You've been given this booklet as an invitation to a very
special church service—a Christmas celebration! It is a time
when we come together in joy, acknowledging the pivotal
point in human history, the birth of Christ, our Savior and
King. It's an amazing time when we remember how God
reached down from heaven and built a bridge between
Himself and those He had so carefully and lovingly crafted in
His own image. The story of that incarnation—God sending
His Son to be born into the human race—is beautiful beyond
our ability to express. We hope what you read in this little
booklet will inspire you to accept our invitation and join
us for this special time of rejoicing. Come hear the timeless
story of an infant king, let your spirit be lifted by the sound
of Christmas carols, and celebrate the miraculous event
that brought us hope, reconciliation with our Creator, and
the promise of an eternity that transcends the bonds of our
earthly existence.*

*The service would only take an hour or two of your time,
and it could be the very thing that adds depth and meaning
to all you do this Christmas. We hope you will come!*

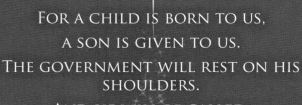

For a child is born to us,
a son is given to us.
The government will rest on his shoulders.
And he will be called:
Wonderful Counselor, Mighty God,
Everlasting Father, Prince of Peace.
His government and its peace
will never end.
He will rule with fairness and justice
from the throne of his ancestor David
for all eternity.
The passionate commitment of the LORD
of Heaven's Armies
will make this happen!

Isaiah 9:6–7 NLT

Christmas

is one of the busiest times of the year. And as time goes by, it's easy to come to think of it less as a joyful celebration of life and more as a time of physical and financial stress. All those parties, all those gifts, all that baking and decorating—what is it all for? It's crazy! As crazy as going all out to celebrate the birthday of someone you don't know all that well or at all.

Christmas is most enjoyed by those who have a keen awareness of the person of Jesus Christ. They not only know the story of His birth and life and death and resurrection, but they know fully what it means to their lives specifically and to all of mankind in general. They understand why one starlit night was different from all the other starlit nights throughout history. They understand why a small town located inauspiciously on Israel's Judean highland was, at least for a moment in time, the most blessed place on earth. They understand why the birth of a child whose parents were simple commoners changed the future of the human race forever. They understand why heavenly angels sang to earthly shepherds and wise men made an arduous journey to a faraway land. And understanding is everything when it comes to Christmas.

Maybe you've never stopped to consider the why of the Christmas season or maybe you know and you've just lost touch with the reason behind the season. Either way, the why is what brings Christmas to life.

PART I

The True Story of Christmas

EVERYTHING CHRISTMAS BEGINS WITH CHRIST!

The Christmas story, recorded in the Bible in the Gospels
of Matthew and Luke, is the foundation for the Christmas
celebration. We would like to share it with you today. If you
decide to attend the Christmas service, hearing the story ahead
of time could greatly enhance your experience. In this first part
of the story, we meet the characters involved and the situations
in which they found themselves. We will meet Elizabeth, who
was to become a mother in her old age, and Mary, her much-
younger relative. We will meet the mighty angel Gabriel, and
Mary's fiancé Joseph. We will hear about the angelic chorus, the
shepherds, and the Magi from the East. We will read about the
priest Simeon and the prophetess Anna. We will learn about the
paranoid King Herod.
**Are you ready to come along with us as we take this
incredible journey?**

THE BIRTH OF JESUS FORETOLD

Luke 1:26–38 NIV

In the sixth month, God sent the angel Gabriel to Nazareth, a
town in Galilee, to a virgin pledged to be married to a man named
Joseph, a descendant of David. The virgin's name was Mary.
The angel went to her and said, "Greetings, you who are highly
favored! The Lord is with you."

Mary was greatly troubled at his words and wondered what
kind of greeting this might be. But the angel said to her, "Do not
be afraid, Mary, you have found favor with God. You will be with
child and give birth to a son, and you are to give him the name
Jesus. He will be great and will be called the Son of the Most
High. The Lord God will give him the throne of his father David,

and he will reign over the house of Jacob forever; his kingdom will never end."

"How will this be," Mary asked the angel, "since I am a virgin?"

The angel answered, "The Holy Spirit will come upon you, and the power of the Most High will overshadow you. So the holy one to be born will be called the Son of God. Even Elizabeth your relative is going to have a child in her old age, and she who was said to be barren is in her sixth month. For nothing is impossible with God."

"I am the Lord's servant," Mary answered. "May it be to me as you have said." Then the angel left her.

—◦◦◇◦◦—

Can you imagine how Mary must have felt? She was a young teenager, probably about fourteen years old, and already pledged in marriage. Her situation could have had terrible implications. Her fiancé, thinking her to be promiscuous, would have rejected her, and the community at large would have shunned her. And yet, Mary accepted with great poise and grace the visit by the angel and the words he spoke to her. Since the angel had mentioned her relative Elizabeth, Mary ran to her side, hoping for comfort and encouragement. As Mary realized the truth of what the angel had said, her joy overflowed in the form of a song to God.

—◦◦◇◦◦—

MARY VISITS ELIZABETH

Luke 1:39–56 NIV

At that time Mary got ready and hurried to a town in the hill country of Judea, where she entered Zechariah's home and greeted Elizabeth. When Elizabeth heard Mary's greeting, the baby leaped in her womb, and Elizabeth was filled with the Holy Spirit. In a loud voice she exclaimed: "Blessed are you among women, and blessed is the child you will bear! But why am I so favored, that the mother of my Lord should come to me? As soon as the sound of your greeting reached my ears, the baby in my womb leaped for joy. Blessed is she who has believed that what the Lord has said to her will be accomplished!"

MARY'S SONG
And Mary said:
"My soul glorifies the Lord
and my spirit rejoices in God
my Savior,
for he has been mindful
of the humble state of his servant.
From now on all generations
will call me blessed,
for the Mighty One has done
great things for me—
holy is his name.
His mercy extends to those
who fear him,
from generation to generation.
He has performed mighty deeds
with his arm;
he has scattered those who are
proud in their inmost thoughts.
He has brought down rulers
from their thrones
but has lifted up the humble.
He has filled the hungry with
good things
but has sent the rich away empty.
He has helped his servant Israel,
remembering to be merciful
to Abraham and his
descendants forever,
even as he said to our fathers."

Mary stayed with Elizabeth for about three months and then returned home.

—•◦•—

Mary must have found great comfort with Elizabeth, knowing that God had revealed to her relative the truth about the child she was carrying. Eventually, she would have to return and face Joseph, her fiancé, and her community. She must have wondered how God would make it right, how He would reveal the truth and clear her name. **Would the angel Gabriel appear again?**

——◦——

THE FAITH OF JOSEPH

Matthew 1:18–25 NIV

This is how the birth of Jesus Christ came about: His mother Mary was pledged to be married to Joseph, but before they came together, she was found to be with child through the Holy Spirit. Because Joseph her husband was a righteous man and did not want to expose her to public disgrace, he had in mind to divorce her quietly.

But after he had considered this, an angel of the Lord appeared to him in a dream and said, "Joseph son of David, do not be afraid to take Mary home as your wife, because what is conceived in her is from the Holy Spirit. She will give birth to a son, and you are to give him the name Jesus, because he will save his people from their sins."

All this took place to fulfill what the Lord had said through the prophet: "The virgin will be with child and will give birth to a son, and they will call him Immanuel"—which means, "God with us."

When Joseph woke up, he did what the angel of the Lord had commanded him and took Mary home as his wife. But he had no union with her until she gave birth to a son. And he gave him the name Jesus.

THE BIRTH OF JESUS

Luke 2:1–20 NIV

In those days Caesar Augustus issued a decree that a census should be taken of the entire Roman world. (This was the first

census that took place while Quirinius was governor of Syria.)
And everyone went to his own town to register.

So Joseph also went up from the town of Nazareth in Galilee to
Judea, to Bethlehem the town of David, because he belonged to
the house and line of David. He went there to register with Mary,
who was pledged to be married to him and was expecting a child.
While they were there, the time came for the baby to be born, and
she gave birth to her firstborn, a son. She wrapped him in cloths
and placed him in a manger, because there was no room for them
in the inn.

THE SHEPHERDS AND THE ANGELS

Luke 2:8-20 NIV

And there were shepherds living out in the fields nearby, keeping
watch over their flocks at night. An angel of the Lord appeared to
them, and the glory of the Lord shone around them, and they were
terrified. But the angel said to them, "Do not be afraid. I bring you
good news of great joy that will be for all the people. Today in the
town of David a Savior has been born to you; he is Christ the Lord.
This will be a sign to you: You will find a baby wrapped in cloths
and lying in a manger."

Suddenly a great company of the heavenly host appeared with
the angel, praising God and saying,
"Glory to God in the highest,
and on earth peace to men
on whom his favor rests."

When the angels had left them and gone into heaven, the
shepherds said to one another, "Let's go to Bethlehem and see
this thing that has happened, which the Lord has told us about."
So they hurried off and found Mary and Joseph, and the baby,
who was lying in the manger. When they had seen him, they
spread the word concerning what had been told them about this
child, and all who heard it were amazed at what the shepherds
said to them. But Mary treasured up all these things and

pondered them in her heart. The shepherds returned, glorifying and praising God for all the things they had heard and seen, which were just as they had been told.

THE VISIT OF THE MAGI (WISE MEN)

Matthew 2:1–12 NIV

After Jesus was born in Bethlehem in Judea, during the time of King Herod, Magi from the east came to Jerusalem and asked, "Where is the one who has been born king of the Jews? We saw his star in the east and have come to worship him."

When King Herod heard this he was disturbed, and all Jerusalem with him. When he had called together all the people's chief priests and teachers of the law, he asked them where the Christ was to be born. "In Bethlehem in Judea," they replied, "for this is what the prophet has written:

" 'But you, Bethlehem, in the land of Judah,
    are by no means least among the rulers of Judah;
for out of you will come a ruler
    who will be the shepherd of my people Israel.' "

Then Herod called the Magi secretly and found out from them the exact time the star had appeared. He sent them to Bethlehem and said, "Go and make a careful search for the child. As soon as you find him, report to me, so that I too may go and worship him."

After they had heard the king, they went on their way, and the star they had seen in the east went ahead of them until it stopped over the place where the child was. When they saw the star, they were overjoyed. On coming to the house, they saw the child with his mother Mary, and they bowed down and worshiped him. Then they opened their treasures and presented him with gifts of gold and of incense and of myrrh. And having been warned in a dream not to go back to Herod, they returned to their country by another route.

—◦—

It would seem that no one who knew of the special events happening that night simply nodded off and fell asleep. Everyone responded in a most dramatic manner. Mary and Joseph responded with humility and released themselves to the purposes of God. The shepherds were awestruck and agreed to leave their flocks and hurry to Bethlehem to see Jesus with their own eyes. The Wise Men from the East were determined to learn the significance of the star they were seeing in the heavens. But old King Herod, hearing of the birth of another king, was anything but overjoyed. He reacted with paranoia and deceit.

How would you have responded to the events of that first Christmas night?

—◦—

JESUS PRESENTED IN THE TEMPLE

Luke 2:21–40 NIV

On the eighth day, when it was time to circumcise him, he was named Jesus, the name the angel had given him before he had been conceived.

When the time of their purification according to the Law of Moses had been completed, Joseph and Mary took him to Jerusalem to present him to the Lord (as it is written in the Law of the Lord, "Every firstborn male is to be consecrated to the Lord"), and to offer a sacrifice in keeping with what is said in the Law of the Lord: "a pair of doves or two young pigeons."

Now there was a man in Jerusalem called Simeon, who was righteous and devout. He was waiting for the consolation of Israel, and the Holy Spirit was upon him. It had been revealed to him by the Holy Spirit that he would not die before he had seen the Lord's Christ. Moved by the Spirit, he went into the temple courts. When the parents brought in the child Jesus to do for him what the custom of the Law required, Simeon took him in his arms and praised God, saying:

"Sovereign Lord, as you have promised,
you now dismiss your servant in peace.
For my eyes have seen your salvation,
which you have prepared in the sight of all people,
a light for revelation to the Gentiles
and for glory to your people Israel."

The child's father and mother marveled at what was said about him. Then Simeon blessed them and said to Mary, his mother: "This child is destined to cause the falling and rising of many in Israel, and to be a sign that will be spoken against, so that the thoughts of many hearts will be revealed. And a sword will pierce your own soul too."

There was also a prophetess, Anna, the daughter of Phanuel, of the tribe of Asher. She was very old; she had lived with her husband seven years after her marriage, and then was a widow until she was eighty-four. She never left the temple but worshiped night and day, fasting and praying. Coming up to them at that very moment, she gave thanks to God and spoke about the child to all who were looking forward to the redemption of Jerusalem.

When Joseph and Mary had done everything required by the Law of the Lord, they returned to Galilee to their own town of Nazareth. And the child grew and became strong; he was filled with wisdom, and the grace of God was upon him.

—◦—

Can you imagine what it must have been like for those who were personally involved in this great God-directed production? They must have felt mystified, awed, honored, and thankful all at once.

What if you had been the simple carpenter asked to accept the unthinkable, a pregnant fiancé? What if you became a mother in your golden years? For those involved, participation in God's plan required "out-on-a-limb" faith. Jeremiah, one of the Old Testament prophets, had spoken about God's promise hundreds of years before, but that must have seemed like a distant connection by the time Mary gave birth on that starry night in Bethlehem. **So ... what were the specifics of that long-ago promise?**

GOD'S PROMISE

In a prophecy recorded in the Bible, Jeremiah said that a descendant of King David would become the promised deliverer or Messiah. He said, "The days are surely coming, says the LORD, when I will raise up for David a righteous Branch, and he shall reign as king and deal wisely, and shall execute justice and righteousness in the land" *(Jeremiah 23:5 NRSV).*

Through another prophet, God gave specific information about the birth of the promised Messiah. Isaiah's words were also recorded in the Bible. He said, "All right then, the Lord himself will give you the sign. Look! The virgin will conceive a child! She will give birth to a son and will call him Immanuel (which means 'God is with us')" *(Isaiah 7:14 NLT).* So this miraculous sign—a child born to a virgin—would indicate that God had once again drawn near to human beings.

Another prophet, Micah, reported that the child would be born in the town of Bethlehem. He said, "But you, Bethlehem Ephrathah, though you are small among the clans of Judah, out of you will come for me one who will be ruler over Israel, whose origins are from of old, from ancient times" *(Micah 5:2 NIV).*

Isn't it wonderful to know that God keeps His promises? He kept the promises He made through the prophets in the Bible, and He will keep the promises He has made to you. Even earthly fathers can't make that claim. They are only human and sooner or later they fail us, but not God. He always does what He says He will do.

WHO WAS
THE CHRIST CHILD?

The world waited with anticipation. And yet, when the Christ Child was born, few recognized Him. The priest Simeon and the prophetess Anna knew who He was as they held Him in their arms, but for most, His true identity was only revealed over time. So who was this tiny infant lying in a manger bed?

Though He looked like a normal, healthy baby, Jesus was far from ordinary. He was in fact the Christ, which means "the anointed one." All human and at the same time all God, He was to serve as a go-between, a bridge between God and His creation. He had been sent to repair the broken relationship between God and man.

John, one of the eyewitnesses to Jesus' life and ministry, verifies the Christ Child's identity. However, the expression of this truth pushed John to the very limits of human language. He wrote, "In the beginning was the Word, and the Word was with God, and the Word was God," and "the Word became flesh and made his dwelling among us" *(John 1:1, 14 NIV)*. Jesus, the eternal expression (Word) of God, had come to live in a human body. Jesus was both divine and human.

Finally! The promise of reconciliation between God and man was being fulfilled.

The book of Hebrews tells us that Jesus' death on the cross, some thirty-three years after His birth, fully satisfied the judgment for and made right the breach sin had caused. "Christ died once for all time as a sacrifice to take away the sins of many people. He will come again, not to deal with our sins, but to bring salvation to all who are eagerly waiting for him" *(Hebrews 9:28 NLT)*.

During Jesus' life on earth, He taught us what it means to be fully human: to have a trusting, open, intimate relationship with God and with others. His words were not without their detractors, however. Eventually, Jesus' enemies succeeded in having Him put to death. But in truth, they were playing right into God's plan. By surrendering His perfect life, Jesus became our Messiah. He traded a perfect life for our lives, scarred and battered by sin. No longer were we identified as children of sin, but now children of God! Just as Adam and Eve walked with God in the Garden of Eden, relishing His fellowship, we were now wrapped, as it were, in His clean white robe and pronounced worthy to stand in His presence—loved and forgiven.

And having given His life, He rose from the grave and conquered the penalties for sin once and for all. No wonder the name, Jesus, means savior. Hallelujah!

What one word best describes your relationship with God right now?

Do you find it interesting that God's plan for mending the breach in our relationship with Him involved the birth of a child? And yet, what better way to bring us back into the family of God? As Jesus Himself put it, we can be born again *(see John 3:3)*. All of us were born once in a physical sense, and all of us need to be reborn spiritually in order to enter this new relationship with God.

We do that by faith, that is, by taking Jesus at His word and placing our confidence in Him. John the apostle said, "But to all who did accept him and believe in him he gave the right to become children of God. They did not become his children in any human way—by any human parents or human desire. They were born of God" *(John 1:12–13 NCV)*.

This is a profound change that goes far deeper than simply deciding to turn over a new leaf. When we accept the sacrifice Jesus made for us on the cross, He sends His Holy Spirit to live within us. The result is that we are able to enter a trusting, honest, secure relationship with the One who created us.

Maybe you've already discovered the true identity of the Christ Child. Maybe you've already made a decision to accept the sacrifice He made for you when He came to earth as a human being, lived a perfect life, and then died in your place on the cross, so that you could be reunited with your heavenly Father. Maybe you already believe that God raised Him up on the third day! If you have, then you already know why a baby born more than two thousand years ago holds critical significance for your life today.

PART II

A Gift for You

However, it's just as possible that you haven't until now fully understood what the events that transpired there in that lowly stable mean for your life in the here and now. If that's the case, ask yourself—are you ready for a new birth? A new beginning?

The greatest gift any of us could hope to receive is not a Christmas present, however grand it might be. It is the gift of new life that God has made possible through His Son, Jesus Christ. This new life is truly a gift. It isn't something you deserve or something you could earn. It's completely free.

Unlike those who had to wait so long for the fulfillment of God's promise, you can receive this gift today. The breach in your relationship with God, your Creator, has already been repaired. All you need to do is open the door of your heart and receive it.

Listen with your heart and you will hear Jesus speaking to you right now. He is saying:

"_____[your name], I came to earth so that you could become part of My family. I love you so much that I was willing to leave My heavenly throne, where I ruled alongside My Father, and took on the flesh and blood body of a human being. I then gave up My earthly life to pay the penalty for your sin and reconcile you with My Father.

"Though My brief stay on earth was more than two thousand years ago, the work I did there is eternal. I am still inviting people to accept the gift of My life. The moment you say yes to Me, you have a warm welcome into the family of God. In fact, you become an adopted son or daughter, and this adoption is complete and final. I become not only your Savior, not only your Lord God, but also your Brother, and My Father becomes your Father, as well.

"Regardless of what words you use, and no matter what difficulties your future may hold, you can now have joy for the rest of your life on earth, because My Holy Spirit will come to live in your heart. And when you die, the door to heaven will be wide open for you. I want nothing more than to spend eternity with you. My Father and I love you more than anybody on earth could possibly love you."

You can pray these words, or use words of your own:

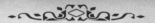

"HEAVENLY FATHER,
I AM AWARE OF A SEPARATION FROM YOU,
AND I KNOW THAT MY SINFULNESS HAS GOTTEN IN THE WAY.
I BELIEVE NOW THAT JESUS CHRIST IS YOUR SON,
AND THAT HE CAME TO EARTH AS A HUMAN
IN ORDER TO TAKE AWAY THE BARRIER OF SIN,
INCLUDING MY OWN.
I BELIEVE THAT WHEN HE SUFFERED AND DIED ON THE
CROSS, HE PAID THE FULL PRICE OF PUNISHMENT FOR SIN.
I BELIEVE THIS MEANS THAT I CAN BE FORGIVEN SO THAT
I CAN COME INTO YOUR HOLY PRESENCE.
"I BELIEVE THAT YOU RAISED JESUS FROM THE DEAD,
PROVING THAT YOUR LIFE IS STRONGER THAN DEATH,
AND THAT THIS OPENED THE WAY TO ETERNAL LIFE FOR ME
AND FOR ANYONE WHO BELIEVES.
WITH ALL OF MY HEART, I WANT TO START OVER;
I WANT TO BE BORN AGAIN.
"I GIVE MY LIFE TO YOU AND I ASK YOU TO TAKE
FULL CONTROL OF IT.
OF MY OWN FREE WILL, I AM MAKING A DECISION TO
FOLLOW YOU, JESUS, AND I THANK YOU FOR INVITING ME
TO COME INTO YOUR FATHER'S FAMILY.
I BELONG TO YOU NOW.
AMEN."

The Bible makes it clear that those who accept Jesus Christ as their Lord and Savior will have all of their sins (past, present, and future) forgiven forever. Take a look at these confirmations from the Bible.

For God so loved the world that He gave His only begotten Son, that whoever believes in Him should not perish but have everlasting life. For God did not send His Son into the world to condemn the world, but that the world through Him might be saved.

John 3:16–17 NKJV

Whoever believes in Him will receive remission of sins.

Acts 10:43 NKJV

He is so rich in kindness and grace that he purchased our freedom with the blood of his Son and forgave our sins.

Ephesians 1:7 NLT

If we confess our sins, he is faithful and just and will forgive us our sins and purify us from all unrighteousness.

1 John 1:9 NIV

Praise the LORD, O my soul, and forget not all his benefits—who forgives all your sins. ... as far as the east is from the west, so far has he removed our transgressions from us.

Psalm 103:2–3, 12 NIV

If you have just accepted Christ, you have something wonderful to celebrate. As is true with all family relationships, your relationship with God will grow stronger as you cultivate the love and trust that began today. Here are some simple things you can do to make that relationship grow.

First, tell someone about your decision to place your faith in Jesus. This will strengthen your desire to live in harmony with Him, and it will be your first opportunity to share the good news with someone else who is hungry for a relationship with God.

Next, begin the daily habit of talking with God through prayer. This can be done anywhere, anytime. Just talk with Him as you would with any person. As you pray and listen reflectively, you will sense God speaking with you too.

Also, begin to feed your mind on the truth of God's Word, the Bible. You can find one at nearly any bookstore, or you can read it free on the Internet. Begin with one of the selections that tell about the life of Jesus, such as the Gospel of John.

Finally, gather with other believers for worship every week. This fellowship will greatly strengthen your faith, and you will be an encouragement to others, as well.

You are part of the family now, the family of God. Happy Birthday!

Who is the first person you will tell about your new life with God?

ALREADY A BELIEVER

As we mentioned earlier, you may already be a member of the family of God. You may have known Jesus for a few years, many years, or even all of your life. Whether you come early or late to the faith, the glorious result is the same. You have been reconciled with God, your heavenly Father.

If you've been a Christian for awhile, though, you may be reluctant to accept our invitation to Christmas service not because you don't understand the significance it holds but because you've had a bad experience with church in the past. It happens more often than any of us would like to admit. Just like any big family, there is going to be conflict at times. In one of his many letters to first-century believers, the Apostle Paul wrote these words: "Be kind and compassionate to one another, forgiving each other, just as in Christ God forgave you" *(Ephesians 4:32 NIV)*.

If there is one word that resonates throughout the Christmas story, it is reconciliation. That involves relationship with God, but it also involves relationship with other Christians. It could be that attending church this Christmas would be a good first step toward re-associating yourself with your brothers and sisters of faith.

Or it could be that your reluctance to go back to church is not nearly so complicated. It could be that you've just gotten busy and now it's tough to fit church into your schedule. Don't worry; you are hardly the first person to drop out of church for lack of time. We live in a society that is always on the move. We spend our days rushing from one thing to another, trying to keep all the plates spinning and responsibilities covered. Many Americans are sleep-deprived, emotionally depleted, and overwhelmed by responsibility. Church seems to be the easiest activity to drop. After all, God is forgiving, right? He isn't going to cut us off because we don't show up. That's true. But think about what is lost when you sacrifice church attendance to your crowded schedule:

1. You miss hearing the life-affirming Word of God read and discussed.
2. You miss the spiritual insights you can obtain from your brothers and sisters in the Lord.
3. You miss joining in with other believers as we praise and worship the Lord together.
4. You miss involving your family in church activities that will help them grow spiritually.
5. You miss the comfort of having a church family during difficult times.
6. You miss having fellowship with those who believe as you do.
7. You miss praying for the needs of others and having others to pray for your needs.
8. You miss sharing your blessings with others and rejoicing as they share their blessings with you.
9. You miss taking part as your local church reaches out to meet the needs of your community.
10. You miss knowing that your children are being nurtured in their relationships with God.

Suffice to say, you miss a lot. **Doesn't it make sense to join us for our Christmas service to remind yourself that church should be at the center of your life rather than on the outskirts?**

WHAT DOES
THE BIBLE SAY?

The Bible makes it clear that going to church is an important part of the believer's life. Take a look at these confirmations from the Bible.

Let us not give up meeting together, as some are in the habit of doing, but let us encourage one another—and all the more as you see the Day approaching.

Hebrews 10:25 NIV

The body we're talking about is Christ's body of chosen people. Each of us finds our meaning and function as a part of his body.

Romans 12:5 MSG

God's household ... is the church of the living God, the pillar and foundation of the truth.

1 Timothy 3:15 NIV

PART III

Come One, Come All

Whether you are a new believer thinking about attending church for the first time or a seasoned believer thinking about going back to church, you may have some practical questions. Let's take a look at some church Q & A.

QUESTION:

What if I go to the Christmas service and I feel invisible—no one talks to me?

Unfortunately, this happens sometimes in churches—even our church. We human beings do tend to get caught up in our own circle of friends and family, and walking up and saying hi to someone new takes effort. But this Christmas season, especially, we have made a commitment to open our eyes and ears and really see those around us. We have been praying for you and that's the first step to successfully reaching out to those outside our familiar church family.

We also understand that we need you. Without new faces in the crowd, it would be easy to become ingrown and lose touch with the exciting things God is doing in the world.

We would also miss out on the special gifting God has placed in your life. It might be your warm smile, your ability to teach the Bible, your practical and spiritual insights, your lovely singing voice, your ability to play a musical instrument. It might be your gift for relating to the older members of our congregation or the younger. There are so many things to be done here in celebration of our renewed relationship with God, and we can't do it nearly as well without the gift that you contribute. The Apostle Paul said it this way: "We have gifts that differ according to the grace given to us: prophecy, in proportion to faith; ministry, in ministering; the teacher, in teaching; the exhorter, in exhortation; the giver, in generosity; the leader, in diligence; the compassionate, in cheerfulness" *(Romans 12:6–8 NRSV)*. We need you as much as you need us! Come and let us prove it to you!

QUESTION:

What if I come to the Christmas service but I'm not ready to commit to joining the church or even coming back for another visit?

We aren't asking for a life-long commitment to attend our church. We would just love to have you come and be part of our Christmas celebration, to worship with us as we commemorate the birth of Christ, our Savior. Of course, we are hopeful that you will come back to visit us again, and we will be delighted if you decide to come on a regular basis and get involved. But you don't need to worry. We won't be tracking you down and demanding to know where you've been. We just want a chance to love you and see if you could be happy here in our church body.

QUESTION:

If I choose not to come to church, does that make me a "bad" person?

Going to church is never about being good or bad. It's about the opportunity to grow in faith, to gain wisdom, to fellowship with people who appreciate mercy and compassion and forgiveness. It does, however, provide a vast array of opportunities to engage in good deeds. The whole purpose of church is to help you become more like Jesus, and He was certainly good. As you learn to live in right relationship with Him, the goodness in your own heart will shine through.

The point here is that church should be a positive influence in your life, a place where positive people do positive things. No one will judge you if you choose not to come, but they will encourage you to keep coming.

QUESTION:

If I do go to church, does that make me a "good" person?

Going to church can't make you good. That's God's work. Church is about helping you grow. Imagine taking a seed and putting it in soil and leaving it there. Will it grow? Probably—in fact, it may even develop into a small shrub with the help of rain, dew, and fresh air. But over time, the shrub will become stunted in its growth. The dead leaves and branches that dry out in the winter will start choking out new growth that wants to start in the spring. These new shoots have nowhere to go, so they will soon get so weak that they will shrivel and die.

What if that shrub had been tended by a gardener who clipped away the dead leaves, pruned the branches, and watered, fed, and nurtured it? It would thrive and probably be in full flower every spring, constantly growing into a bigger and bigger masterpiece in the garden. Its roots would go down deep and spread wide, and it would be established and healthy. You may well be aware of some dead leaves and stunted growth in your own life. Maybe it's time to bring your shrub back to the gardener for some tending.

If you think this metaphor sounds familiar, it should. In this way, Jesus taught us about the importance of abiding (remaining) in Him. God is our gardener, Jesus is like the vine, and we are the branches. How can a branch sustain itself if it's not connected to the vine?

[Jesus replied:] "I am the true vine, and my Father is the gardener. He cuts off every branch in me that bears no fruit, while every branch that does bear fruit he prunes so that it will be even more fruitful. You are already clean because of the word I have spoken to you. Remain in me, and I will remain in you. No branch can bear fruit by itself; it must remain in the vine. Neither can you bear fruit unless you remain in me. I am the vine; you are the branches. If a man remains in me and I in him, he will bear much fruit; apart from me you can do nothing. If anyone does not remain in me, he is like a branch that is thrown away and withers; such branches are picked up, thrown into the fire and burned. If you remain in me and my words remain in you, ask whatever you wish, and it will be given you."

John 15:1–7 NIV

QUESTION:

If I come for the Christmas service is someone going to pressure me to give money to the church?

Your concern is understandable. Churches are notorious for passing the offering plate up and down aisles filled with a captive audience. We don't mean to put pressure on you though. The intention is just to provide for our church needs, while providing an opportunity for you to give something to God and receive His blessing. We have learned that you can never out-give God. He always gives back so much more than we give to Him.

Just the same, we can assure you that taking an offering is not by any means the central priority when we gather to worship. That is especially true for the Christmas service. Furthermore, we would never judge you for exercising your choice to give or not to give. You would be, first and foremost, our guest. So leave your wallet at home. We want you—not your money.

QUESTION:

What if the sermon is boring?

If you decide to join us for our Christmas service, we guarantee it won't be boring! How could it be? How could the carol singing and the story of the most exciting moment in human history be boring?

We'll be honest, however. Should you choose to visit us regularly, you may not find every sermon to be as inspiring. For one thing, you may have limited understanding concerning the principles conveyed from the pulpit. You might not be familiar with the Bible characters or their situations. You might not be spiritually ready to digest all the preacher has to say.

What you may not know, however, is that this is a challenge for all of us. We've all come into this church at various levels of spiritual growth. Some of us learned the Bible stories in our childhood; others never entered a church building until we were grown. We've found that as we grow in our faith, we become more and more interested in what is being said by the preacher. For example, quantum physics is an amazing field, very exciting with its mind-bending theories and physical predictions. But individuals who have not studied the science might find it difficult to sit through a lecture on the subject. They would be unfamiliar with the terminology and the basic concepts that undergird the speaker's remarks. Only as they begin to learn and understand the science involved would their interest be piqued.

Of course, realistically, some of us may never be capable of learning about and enjoying such an advanced field of science. But God has guaranteed that all of us will be able to learn and master the principles of the Christian faith. When we become believers, the Holy Spirit comes into our hearts and minds and takes up residence. He is the one who helps us grow spiritually. He tutors us in our God understanding. In the Gospel of John *(John 14:26)*, Jesus said to His followers: "But the Counselor, the Holy Spirit, whom the Father will send in my name, will teach you all things and will remind you of everything I have said to you."

We hope by now you've decided to accept our invitation to worship with us during our Christmas service. But just in case you need more convincing, here are ten good reasons to come join us!

1. You remember Christmas services from your childhood and would like to re-connect with those memories.
2. You would like to make the beauty and pageantry of the Christmas story a part of your annual Christmas activities.
3. You want your children to hear the Christmas story and be reminded that Christmas is about more than getting gifts and leaving treats for Santa.
4. You want to be with people during this emotional, and often lonely, season.
5. You want to be somewhere peaceful and holy as you meditate on the significance of this special time.
6. You enjoy singing those beautiful Christmas carols in the glow of candlelight.
7. You've been thinking about going back to church anyway, and this would be a good time to do it.
8. You would like to get to know the person who gave you this booklet and accepting his or her invitation would be the first step to doing that.
9. Being in church on Christmas helps you relax from the stress of the season.
10. You've been longing for a touch from God and it seems like this would be a great time to reach out to Him.

We've done all we can to convince you to attend our Christmas service. Even if you're sold though, you may still have some practical concerns like these:

QUESTION:

What should I wear?

We can assure you, it will not be necessary to go out and buy yourself something fancy to wear to our Christmas service or to any other service for that matter. Sure, some people will dress up just because it is a custom for them to do so for this special occasion. If that's what you feel comfortable doing, feel free to add to the sense of pageantry for the evening.

On the other hand, you may not be the type of person who likes to dress up and that's quite all right, too! Even for holiday services, it's acceptable to dress more casually and comfortably. No one will be calling the fashion police to complain about you or judging you for what you choose to wear. The only thing we ask is to dress modestly out of respect for the Lord.

QUESTION:

What time should I be there?

For the Christmas service, it would be a good idea to get to the church fifteen or twenty minutes early to get a good seat, especially if you are coming with your family and loved ones. Coming too early though might cause you to interrupt the choir or pageant rehearsal. And the greeters might not yet be in place to answer your questions or show you around.

If you decide to come back to visit for a regular service, you should plan to be there about ten minutes early. This will give you time to drop off your children in the nursery, decide where in the sanctuary you are most comfortable sitting, and meet a few of your fellow churchgoers.

We hope you won't choose not to come because you're running a few minutes late or have to arrive after the service has started for some reason. The doors of our church remain open throughout the service and you are welcome to join us at any time.

QUESTION:

Should I try to meet new people or just stay under the radar?

This is entirely your choice. Sometimes, it's less threatening to keep a low profile on the first visit. Simply be polite, and introduce yourself if asked. If someone asks if it's your first time, it's OK to tell the person that you're "just visiting." Don't feel obliged to engage if you're not comfortable. Be open to meeting at least one new person, though. It will be easier to return if you can expect to see a familiar face.

One more thing, the Christmas service is one time during the year when families tend to sit together. It's a great time to see who belongs to whom and make connections between parents and children, sisters and brothers, and even grandparents and their clans.

QUESTION:

Is there anything I need to bring?

If you have a Bible, bring it along so you can follow the Scriptures used in the sermon. But if you don't have a Bible, no worries. We have plenty and we would be glad to share if you ask.

QUESTION:

How should I act?

All churches have their own ways of doing things, and this can seem scary at first when you're not sure what, when, or how to do these things. The best plan is to watch others around you. Regular attendees will know the routine, so follow their lead. If something seems weird or you don't understand it, just go with the flow. It will make sense eventually, and you can't be expected to know at first. You shouldn't feel obliged to participate in any aspect of the service that makes you uncomfortable, and it is OK to stay in your seat when others may stand up to sing or move to the front for prayer.

Remember your first day at a new school? You probably came that first day feeling a little insecure about what would be expected of you. But before long, you were well-versed in how things were supposed to be done. Church protocol is no different. Of course, we'd like you to remember the usual courtesies like turning off your cell phone, keeping your voice low if you have to speak to someone, and letting our nursery help you if your baby or small child is acting up. Other than that, there aren't any "rules." We just want you to relax and enjoy yourself.

QUESTION:

Should I respond to the request for follow-up information?

The Christmas service may be an exception, but if you choose to visit us again, you may be asked to fill out an information card. We hope you won't feel intimidated by this. No one is going to knock on your door unannounced or ask you for money or obligate you in any other way. But wouldn't it be sad if you came and visited us and no one ever wrote down your name or had a record that you were there?

Just know that if you decide to come it will mean a lot to us, and we will want to have an opportunity to introduce ourselves to you and find out a little about you. Sometimes, there isn't a chance for everyone to do that before or after the service. We want to do more than notice your face in the crowd. We want to remember you in our prayers and recognize your name if you should call for help sometime in the future. We want to be able to let you know when our congregation is doing something special that you might want to be part of. So ... no penalty for refusing to give us your information, but we hope you will.

The most important tip of all?

Be yourself! Come with an open heart and mind, and we are sure God will meet you here. We promise to do our best to make it a good experience for you, but there's no doubt what God will do. He will be waiting to bless you, comfort you, renew you, restore you, and fill you with joy. We hope this will be the very best Christmas in your life so far. We pray that Jesus, the risen Christ who was sent to earth as a baby, will become the central figure in your Christmas story.

Until then, we hope you will be blessed by the words of this wonderful Christmas hymn extracted from the carol "Hark the Herald Angels Sing" and sung to the same tune. It was written by Charles Wesley, with music composed by Felix Mendelssohn.
Merry Christmas!

CHRIST WAS BORN IN BETHLEHEM

CHRIST, BY HIGHEST HEAVEN ADORED
CHRIST, THE EVERLASTING LORD;
LATE IN TIME BEHOLD HIM COME
OFFSPRING OF A VIRGIN'S WOMB.
VEILED IN FLESH THE GODHEAD SEE;
HAIL TH' INCARNATE DEITY,
PLEASED AS MAN WITH MAN TO DWELL;
JESUS, OUR EMMANUEL.

COME, DESIRE OF NATIONS COME,
FIX IN US THY HUMBLE HOME;
RISE, THE WOMAN'S CONQUERING SEED,
BRUISE IN US THE SERPENT'S HEAD.
ADAM'S LIKENESS, LORD EFFACE:
STAMP THY IMAGE IN ITS PLACE;
SECOND ADAM, FROM ABOVE,
REINSTATE US IN THY LOVE.

HAIL, THE HEAV'N-BORN PRINCE OF PEACE!
HAIL, THE SON OF RIGHTEOUSNESS!
LIGHT AND LIFE TO ALL HE BRINGS,
RIS'N WITH HEALING IN HIS WINGS.
MILD HE LAYS HIS GLORY BY,
BORN THAT MAN NO MORE MAY DIE,
BORN TO RAISE THE SONS OF EARTH.
BORN TO GIVE THEM SECOND BIRTH.